The Rules of Crypto

ABRAHAM ADESEYE

Copyright © 2025 Abraham Adeseye

All rights reserved

DEDICATION

To the visionaries, creators, and pioneers who are shaping the future of finance and technology, your innovation continues to inspire and drive the world forward.

To those who believe in the power of blockchain, cryptocurrency, and NFTs to create new possibilities and opportunities for all—this book is for you. May it serve as a guide on your journey through the evolving digital landscape.

And to my readers, thank you for your curiosity and commitment to understanding the complexities of this transformative space. The future is in your hands, and with knowledge, strategy, and innovation, you have the power to shape it.

Contents

Introduction

1 : Understanding the Foundations

2 The Golden Rule: DYOR (Do Your Own Research)

3 Security First

4 Diversification and Risk Management

5 Mastering Market Dynamics

6 Timing the Market vs. Time in the Market

7 Identifying High-Potential Crypto Projects

8 The Psychology of Crypto Investing

9 Crypto Trading Strategies

10 Securing Your Crypto Assets

11 Maximizing Long-Term Growth in Crypto Investments

12 Navigating the Tax Implications of Crypto Investments

13 The Future of Crypto and Long-Term Success

14 The Future of NFTs

Conclusion: Embracing the Future of Crypto

Introduction

Cryptocurrency is one of the most groundbreaking innovations of the 21st century, revolutionizing the way we think about money, value, and ownership. Born from a desire to create a decentralized, secure, and transparent financial system, cryptocurrencies like Bitcoin and Ethereum have challenged traditional norms and opened doors to opportunities that were once unimaginable.

Yet, with great opportunity comes great complexity. The crypto world is a landscape of rapid change, massive potential, and significant risk. For every success story of individuals amassing wealth, there are countless tales of loss, confusion, and regret. The volatile nature of cryptocurrencies, combined with a lack of universal regulation and widespread misinformation, has made this space both exciting and intimidating.

This book, *The Rules of Crypto*, is designed to be your compass in navigating this ever-evolving world. Whether you're a curious newcomer or an experienced investor looking to refine your strategies, the rules laid out in these pages will serve as your foundation for success.

You'll learn not only the technical aspects of how cryptocurrencies work but also the mindset, strategies, and tools you need to make informed decisions. From understanding blockchain basics to mastering advanced trading techniques, this book offers practical insights and actionable advice to help you thrive in this dynamic environment.

Cryptocurrency isn't just about making money; it's about being part of a global movement that's reshaping industries, empowering individuals, and redefining the future of finance. With the right knowledge and approach, you can harness this potential to build wealth and make a meaningful impact.

Welcome to the exciting world of crypto. Let's unlock its possibilities together.

1 : Understanding the Foundations

To navigate the world of cryptocurrency effectively, it is essential to start with a strong understanding of its foundations. What exactly is cryptocurrency? How does it work? Why does it matter? These are the questions we'll address in this chapter as we explore the origins, mechanics, and potential of this revolutionary technology.

What Is Cryptocurrency?

At its core, cryptocurrency is digital money. However, unlike traditional currencies such as the US Dollar or Euro, cryptocurrencies operate on decentralized networks, meaning they are not controlled by any government or central authority. Instead, they rely on blockchain technology, a distributed ledger system that ensures security, transparency, and immutability.

Bitcoin, introduced in 2009 by an anonymous entity known as Satoshi Nakamoto, was the first cryptocurrency. It was designed as a peer-to-peer electronic cash system, enabling users to send and receive payments without intermediaries like banks. Since then, thousands of cryptocurrencies have been created, each with its unique purpose and use case.

The Birth of Bitcoin and the Rise of Altcoins

The creation of Bitcoin marked the beginning of a financial revolution. Initially dismissed as a fringe technology, Bitcoin steadily gained traction as people began to recognize its potential to disrupt traditional finance.

Following Bitcoin's success, a wave of alternative cryptocurrencies, or "altcoins," emerged. Ethereum introduced the concept of smart contracts, enabling developers to build decentralized applications (DApps) on its blockchain. Other notable cryptocurrencies like Litecoin, Cardano, and Solana brought unique innovations, from faster transaction speeds to enhanced scalability.

The Role of Blockchain Technology

Blockchain is the backbone of cryptocurrency. It is a decentralized, digital ledger that records all transactions across a network of computers. Each transaction is grouped into a "block," and these blocks are linked together chronologically, forming a "chain."

Key features of blockchain technology include:

- **Decentralization:** No single entity has control over the network.
- **Transparency:** Transactions are visible to all participants on the network.
- **Immutability:** Once data is recorded on the blockchain, it cannot be altered or deleted.

This combination of features ensures that cryptocurrencies are secure, efficient, and resistant to fraud.

How Cryptocurrencies Are Created

Cryptocurrencies can be created through processes like mining or staking, depending on the blockchain's underlying consensus mechanism:

- **Mining:** In proof-of-work (PoW) systems like Bitcoin, mining involves solving complex mathematical problems to validate transactions and add them to the blockchain. Miners are rewarded with newly minted coins.
- **Staking:** In proof-of-stake (PoS) systems like Ethereum 2.0, participants lock up their cryptocurrency as collateral to validate transactions. Stakers earn rewards for securing the network without the need for energy-intensive mining.

Why Cryptocurrency Matters

Cryptocurrency is more than just a speculative investment. It has real-world applications that address key issues in traditional finance and beyond, such as:

- **Financial Inclusion:** Cryptocurrencies provide access to financial services for billions of people worldwide who are unbanked or underbanked.
- **Cross-Border Payments:** Transactions are faster, cheaper, and more transparent compared to traditional banking systems.
- **Decentralization:** By removing the need for intermediaries, cryptocurrencies empower individuals to have full control over their money.

Challenges and Opportunities

While the potential of cryptocurrency is immense, it is not without challenges. Volatility, regulatory uncertainty, and security risks remain significant barriers to widespread adoption. However, as technology advances and regulations become clearer, the opportunities for growth and innovation are limitless.

Conclusion

Understanding the basics of cryptocurrency is the first step to unlocking its potential. By grasping its origins, technology, and applications, you can build a solid foundation for exploring the opportunities this revolutionary space has to offer.

2 The Golden Rule: DYOR (Do Your Own Research)

In the fast-moving and often confusing world of cryptocurrency, the mantra "Do Your Own Research" (DYOR) is not just advice—it's a survival skill. With thousands of projects, coins, and tokens in the market, separating legitimate opportunities from scams requires critical thinking, skepticism, and a methodical approach to research.

This chapter explores why DYOR is essential, how to conduct effective research, and the common pitfalls to avoid.

Why Research Is Critical in Crypto Investing

Unlike traditional financial markets, the cryptocurrency space lacks widespread regulation and oversight. This decentralized nature, while empowering, also creates an environment ripe for misinformation, scams, and pump-and-dump schemes.

Without proper research, you risk investing in:

- **Overhyped projects** that have no real utility or long-term potential.
- **Scams** designed to steal your funds.
- **Volatile assets** that could wipe out your investment overnight.
-

By doing your own research, you can make informed decisions, minimize risks, and identify opportunities that align with your goals.

How to Conduct Effective Research

1. **Understand the Basics of a Project**

   Before investing in any cryptocurrency, start with these key questions:
   - What problem does the project aim to solve?
   - What is the utility of its token?

- Who are the founders and developers?
- Does the project have a working product, or is it still in development?

Begin by visiting the project's official website, reading its whitepaper, and understanding its mission and roadmap.

2. **Evaluate the Team**

    A strong, transparent, and experienced team is often a sign of a credible project. Research the backgrounds of the founders and developers:
    - Are they reputable in the crypto or tech community?
    - Do they have a track record of successful ventures?
    - Are they active and engaging with the community?

3. **Analyze the Technology**

    A cryptocurrency project is only as strong as its underlying technology. Dive into the technical aspects:
    - Is the project built on a secure and scalable blockchain?
    - What consensus mechanism does it use (e.g., proof of work, proof of stake)?
    - Is the code open source, allowing for transparency and community contributions?

4. **Assess Market Data**

    Market performance can offer valuable insights into a cryptocurrency's potential. Look for:
    - **Market Capitalization:** Indicates the overall value of a cryptocurrency.
    - **Trading Volume:** High volume suggests strong investor interest and liquidity.
    - **Circulating Supply vs. Total Supply:** Determines how much of the token is already in circulation.

5. **Community Engagement**

   A thriving and engaged community is often a good indicator of a project's health. Check platforms like Twitter, Reddit, Discord, and Telegram to gauge:

   - How active the community is.
   - Whether the team communicates regularly and transparently.
   - The quality of discussions—are they constructive or overly promotional?

6. **Read Independent Reviews and Analyses**

   While official sources are helpful, independent reviews can provide unbiased perspectives. Look for reviews from reputable analysts, YouTubers, and bloggers who focus on cryptocurrency. Be wary of overly positive reviews, as they may be sponsored content.

Common Red Flags to Watch Out For

1. **Guaranteed Returns**

   Any project that promises guaranteed returns is likely a scam. The crypto market is highly volatile, and no investment is risk-free.

2. **Anonymous Teams**

   While some legitimate projects are run by anonymous teams, this can be a red flag. Transparency builds trust.

3. **No Real-World Use Case**

   A project with no practical application or value proposition is unlikely to succeed in the long term.

4. **Unrealistic Roadmaps**

   Overly ambitious goals with tight deadlines often indicate poor planning or outright deception.

5. **Aggressive Marketing**

   Projects that rely heavily on hype, giveaways, or celebrity endorsements may lack substance.

Tools and Resources for Research

- **CoinMarketCap and CoinGecko:** Platforms for tracking market data and token performance.
- **Etherscan and BscScan:** Blockchain explorers for verifying transactions and token details.
- **Whitepapers:** Detailed documents explaining a project's purpose and mechanics.
- **Crypto News Sites:** Stay updated with credible sources like CoinDesk and The Block.
- **Social Media:** Follow official project accounts and join community discussions on Twitter, Reddit, and Telegram.

The Importance of Independent Thinking

While it's valuable to consider the opinions of experts and influencers, always form your own conclusions. Herd mentality can lead to bad decisions, especially during periods of market hype or panic. Trust your research and remain objective.

Conclusion

Doing your own research is the golden rule of crypto investing. It empowers you to make informed decisions, protect your assets, and identify genuine opportunities in a market filled with uncertainty. With a structured approach to research and a keen eye for detail, you can confidently navigate the complexities of the crypto space.

3 Security First

In the cryptocurrency world, security isn't optional—it's essential. Unlike traditional financial systems, where banks and financial institutions can offer recourse for fraud or theft, cryptocurrency transactions are final and irreversible. This makes protecting your assets and information paramount.

In this chapter, we'll explore the best practices for safeguarding your crypto investments, including wallet management, private key protection, and recognizing potential threats.

The Importance of Security in Crypto

Cryptocurrencies operate on decentralized networks, which eliminate intermediaries and offer users full control of their funds. While this is empowering, it also comes with responsibility. If your private keys are lost or stolen, you lose access to your funds—forever.

The crypto ecosystem is also a frequent target for hackers and scammers due to its anonymous nature and lack of regulation. By prioritizing security, you can protect yourself from these threats and ensure the safety of your investments.

Understanding Wallets: Hot vs. Cold

Crypto wallets are the tools you use to store and manage your digital assets. There are two main types: **hot wallets** and **cold wallets**.
1. **Hot Wallets**
    - Connected to the internet, making them

convenient for frequent transactions.
    - Examples: Mobile wallets, desktop wallets, and web wallets.
    - Risks: More vulnerable to hacking due to their constant online presence.
    - Best For: Small amounts of crypto used for trading or spending.
2. **Cold Wallets**
    - Stored offline, providing maximum security against online threats.
    - Examples: Hardware wallets (e.g., Ledger, Trezor) and paper wallets.
    - Risks: Can be lost or damaged if not stored properly.
    - Best For: Long-term storage of large amounts of cryptocurrency.

Rule of Thumb: Use a combination of both wallet types. Keep small amounts in hot wallets for everyday use and store the majority of your assets in cold wallets.

Protecting Your Private Keys

Private keys are the most critical aspect of your cryptocurrency security. They grant access to your funds and are required to authorize transactions.

Tips for Protecting Your Private Keys:

1. **Never Share Them:** Treat your private keys like the PIN to your bank account—private and confidential.
2. **Use Secure Storage:** Store them in a safe place, such as a password-protected file or a secure physical location.
3. **Backup Regularly:** Keep multiple backups of your private keys in separate, secure locations.
4. **Avoid Cloud Storage:** Storing private keys in the cloud can expose them to hacks or unauthorized access.

Securing Your Accounts

Beyond wallets, your crypto exchange accounts and other related platforms also require robust security measures.

Steps to Secure Your Accounts:

1. **Enable Two-Factor Authentication (2FA):** Use apps like Google Authenticator for an additional layer of security.
2. **Use Strong, Unique Passwords:** Avoid reusing passwords across platforms. A password manager can help you create and store strong passwords.
3. **Monitor Account Activity:** Regularly check for unauthorized access or suspicious activity.
4. **Whitelist Withdrawal Addresses:** Restrict withdrawals to a list of pre-approved wallet addresses.

Recognizing and Avoiding Scams

Scammers in the crypto space are constantly evolving their tactics. Being aware of common schemes can help you avoid falling victim to fraud.

Common Scams and How to Avoid Them:

1. **Phishing Scams:** Fake websites or emails designed to steal your credentials.
    - Always verify the URL of any site you log into.
    - Never click on links from unsolicited emails or messages.
2. **Pump-and-Dump Schemes:** Coordinated efforts to inflate a token's price, then sell off holdings.
    - Avoid coins promoted heavily on social media without credible backing.
3. **Fake Giveaways:** Scams that promise free crypto in

exchange for a small "verification" payment.
- Legitimate giveaways never require you to send funds first.
4. **Malicious Apps or Software:** Fake wallets or trading apps that steal your private keys.
   - Only download apps from official sources.
5. **Impersonation Scams:** Fraudsters posing as customer support or crypto influencers.
   - Legitimate representatives will never ask for your private keys or passwords.

Advanced Security Measures

For those with significant holdings or a deep involvement in crypto, advanced security measures can offer extra protection:

1. **Multi-Signature Wallets:** Require multiple private keys to authorize transactions, adding an additional layer of security.
2. **Hardware Security Modules (HSMs):** Specialized devices for secure key storage and management.
3. **Dedicated Devices:** Use a separate, clean device solely for crypto transactions to minimize exposure to malware.

Staying Updated

The crypto landscape is constantly evolving, and so are the threats. Stay informed by:

- Following reputable crypto security blogs and news sites.
- Participating in community forums to learn about emerging threats.
- Regularly updating your wallets, apps, and devices to the latest versions.

Conclusion

Security is the foundation of success in cryptocurrency. By understanding wallet types, protecting your private keys, and staying vigilant against scams, you can safeguard your investments in this high-stakes digital world.

As you continue your crypto journey, remember that security isn't a one-time effort—it's an ongoing process.

4 Diversification and Risk Management

In cryptocurrency, one rule stands out above all: never put all your eggs in one basket. The crypto market is notorious for its volatility, where fortunes can be made and lost in minutes. Diversification and risk management are essential strategies to protect your portfolio and achieve long-term success.

In this chapter, we'll explore how to diversify your investments, manage risk effectively, and make rational decisions in a highly emotional market.

What Is Diversification?

Diversification is the practice of spreading your investments across different assets to reduce risk. In the context of crypto, this means holding a mix of cryptocurrencies with varying purposes, sectors, and risk levels.

The goal is simple: if one investment underperforms, others can help balance your portfolio.

Why Diversification Matters in Crypto

The cryptocurrency market is highly unpredictable. Factors like regulatory news, technological updates, and market sentiment can lead to sudden price swings. By diversifying:

- You minimize the impact of poor performance from any single investment.
- You position yourself to benefit from growth in different areas of the crypto ecosystem.
- You reduce emotional decision-making, as your portfolio isn't overly reliant on one asset.

How to Diversify Your Crypto Portfolio

1. **Invest Across Market Categories**

    Cryptocurrencies serve different purposes. Diversify by investing in:

    - **Store of Value:** Assets like Bitcoin, often called "digital gold."
    - **Smart Contract Platforms:** Examples include Ethereum, Solana, and Cardano.
    - **DeFi (Decentralized Finance):** Tokens like Aave, Uniswap, and MakerDAO.
    - **Utility Tokens:** Cryptos used within specific ecosystems, like Chainlink or Filecoin.
    - **Meme Coins or High-Risk Tokens:** Such as Dogecoin or Shiba Inu (allocate only a small portion).

2. **Balance Risk Levels**

    Categorize assets based on their risk:

    - **Low-Risk:** Established cryptocurrencies like Bitcoin and Ethereum.
    - **Medium-Risk:** Emerging projects with strong use cases.
    - **High-Risk:** New or speculative tokens with high potential but little track record.

    Allocate your investments based on your risk tolerance and goals.

3. **Diversify by Geography**

    Explore projects based on their geographical focus.

Different regions may face unique regulations and market dynamics, affecting token performance.

4. **Allocate Between Crypto and Other Assets**

   Crypto should be part of a broader investment strategy. Diversify further by holding:

   - Traditional assets like stocks, bonds, and real estate.
   - Stablecoins like USDT or USDC for liquidity and stability.
   - Precious metals like gold or silver for long-term security.

Risk Management Strategies

Diversification is only one part of risk management. To navigate the volatile crypto market effectively, adopt these strategies:

1. **Invest What You Can Afford to Lose**
   Never invest money you can't afford to lose. The crypto market is unpredictable, and even the best projects carry inherent risks.
2. **Set a Budget**
   Define how much of your overall portfolio will be allocated to crypto. Many experts recommend no more than 10-20% of your total investments, depending on your risk tolerance.
3. **Use Stop-Loss Orders**
   A stop-loss order automatically sells your asset if it drops to a specified price, limiting potential losses. Most exchanges allow you to set these to protect your investments.
4. **Rebalance Your Portfolio Regularly**

As prices fluctuate, your portfolio allocation may change. Periodically rebalance your holdings to maintain your desired level of risk.

5. **Limit Leverage**
   While leverage can amplify gains, it can also lead to significant losses. Use leverage cautiously, if at all.
6. **Avoid Emotional Trading**
   Fear and greed are the two biggest enemies of crypto investors. Stick to your plan, avoid chasing pumps, and don't panic sell during market dips.

Common Mistakes to Avoid

1. **Over-Diversification**
   While diversification is essential, spreading yourself too thin can dilute your gains and make portfolio management challenging. Focus on quality over quantity.
2. **Ignoring Research**
   Diversification doesn't mean randomly picking assets. Each investment should be backed by thorough research and a clear rationale.
3. **FOMO (Fear of Missing Out)**
   Don't buy into projects just because they're trending. Hype often leads to inflated prices and can result in significant losses when the bubble bursts.
4. **Neglecting Stablecoins**
   Stablecoins provide a safe haven during market turbulence. Always keep a portion of your portfolio in stable assets for flexibility and risk reduction.

Creating a Balanced Portfolio

Here's an example of a diversified crypto portfolio based on risk levels:
- **50% Low-Risk:** Bitcoin, Ethereum

- **30% Medium-Risk:** Solana, Polkadot, Chainlink
- **10% High-Risk:** Emerging or speculative tokens
- **10% Stablecoins:** USDT, USDC

Adjust this allocation based on your risk tolerance, market knowledge, and investment goals.

Case Study: A Tale of Two Investors

Consider two hypothetical investors:

- **Investor A** puts all their money into a single, high-risk altcoin. When the project fails, they lose everything.
- **Investor B** diversifies across multiple assets and sectors. While some investments underperform, others thrive, leading to steady overall growth.

The lesson is clear: diversification and risk management are your best defences in the unpredictable world of crypto.

Conclusion

Diversification and risk management are not just strategies—they're necessities for thriving in the cryptocurrency market. By spreading your investments, maintaining discipline, and preparing for volatility, you can build a portfolio that withstands market fluctuations and grows over time.

5 Mastering Market Dynamics

The world of cryptocurrency is dynamic, fast-paced, and highly volatile. Understanding the fundamental forces that drive market behaviour is essential for anyone looking to succeed as a crypto investor. While market dynamics can be unpredictable, recognizing the patterns, the key players, and the factors that influence price movements will give you a distinct edge. In this chapter, we will dive into how you can master market dynamics, equipping you with the knowledge to make informed decisions and navigate the complexities of the crypto market.

Understanding Crypto Market Drivers

At the core of any financial market lies a set of drivers that influence price movements. In the crypto world, these drivers are unique due to the decentralized nature of digital assets, the lack of centralized control, and the involvement of a wide variety of global participants. Let's explore the primary market drivers in cryptocurrency:

1. **Supply and Demand:**

    Like any asset class, supply and demand are the fundamental forces that drive price movements. The limited supply of many cryptocurrencies, particularly Bitcoin, plays a significant role in this. For instance, Bitcoin has a capped supply of 21 million coins, which creates scarcity. When demand for Bitcoin increases, prices rise due to this limited supply.

    Similarly, the demand for altcoins is influenced by factors such as technological innovation, partnerships, community adoption, and real-world use cases. Understanding the market's overall supply and demand cycle is crucial to anticipating price fluctuations.

2. **Market Sentiment:**

   Sentiment in the crypto market is often driven by news, social media, and public perception. Positive sentiment, such as announcements from major corporations adopting Bitcoin or favourable regulatory news, can lead to rapid price increases. Conversely, negative sentiment, such as regulatory crackdowns, hacks, or market crashes, can cause sharp declines.

Investor sentiment in crypto is more volatile than in traditional markets due to the emotional nature of many retail investors. This can lead to "FOMO" (fear of missing out) during bull markets and panic selling during bear markets. By analyzing market sentiment through platforms like Twitter, Reddit, and other crypto forums, you can gain insights into the mood of the market and make more informed decisions.

3. **Technological Developments and Updates:**

   The crypto market is driven by technological advancements. Major updates, such as network upgrades (hard forks or soft forks), new project releases, or innovations in blockchain technology, can have a profound impact on the value of a cryptocurrency. For example, Ethereum's transition from Proof of Work (PoW) to Proof of Stake (PoS) through the Ethereum 2.0 upgrade significantly altered its network dynamics and price behaviour.

Staying updated on the latest technological trends and developments in the crypto world is crucial. Whether it's the launch of a new decentralized finance (DeFi) protocol or the introduction of privacy features in a blockchain, these developments can provide opportunities or signal risks.

4. **Market Liquidity:**

   Liquidity refers to the ability to buy or sell an asset without significantly affecting its price. High liquidity in a crypto asset typically results in smoother price movements, while low liquidity can lead to more volatile fluctuations. Liquidity can be influenced by factors such as the number of buyers and sellers, the volume of trades, and the market capitalization of the coin.

   For smaller or less well-known altcoins, liquidity can be a major concern. In markets with low liquidity, prices can be easily manipulated by large holders, also known as "whales," who control significant portions of the asset.

5. **Whales and Large Institutions:**

   "Whales" are large investors or entities that hold a significant amount of a particular cryptocurrency. These players can manipulate market prices due to their large holdings. They can buy or sell massive amounts of crypto, influencing the market in ways that individual retail investors cannot.

   In addition to whales, large institutions—like hedge funds, corporations, and even countries—are increasingly entering the crypto space. Their involvement can dramatically impact the market's direction. For instance, when Tesla announced it had purchased $1.5 billion in Bitcoin, the market saw a significant price increase. Understanding the behaviour of whales and institutions is key to predicting market movements.

Key Concepts in Crypto Market Behaviour

To become a master of crypto market dynamics, you need to understand specific concepts that drive market behaviour:

1. **Market Cycles:** Like any asset class, cryptocurrencies follow market cycles: periods of growth (bull markets) followed by periods of decline (bear markets). These cycles can be triggered by a variety of factors, including technological advancements, macroeconomic events, or shifts in sentiment.
   - **Bull Markets:** Characterized by rising prices, increased investor confidence, and widespread media coverage. In these periods, more people enter the market, which pushes prices higher.
   - **Bear Markets:** Characterized by falling prices, uncertainty, and a retreat of investors from the market. During bear markets, prices can experience sharp declines as fear and pessimism dominate investor behaviour.
   - **Accumulation Phases:** These are periods between bull and bear markets when prices stabilize, and long-term investors "accumulate" assets at lower prices before the next bull run. Understanding accumulation phases allows you to spot opportunities before prices surge.

2. **Technical Analysis (TA):**
   Technical analysis involves studying past price movements, chart patterns, and volume to predict future market behaviour. The goal is to identify trends, support and resistance levels, and potential breakout points. By mastering TA, you can anticipate market shifts and capitalize on price movements. Some common tools and indicators used in TA include:
   - **Candlestick Charts:** Visual representations of price

movements over a specific period.
- **Moving Averages:** Help identify trends and smooth out price data to identify support or resistance levels.
- **Relative Strength Index (RSI):** A momentum oscillator that helps identify overbought or oversold conditions.

3. **Fundamental Analysis (FA):**
   While technical analysis focuses on past price movements, fundamental analysis (FA) looks at the core value of a cryptocurrency, including factors such as:
   - **The Development Team:** A strong, experienced team behind a project often signals long-term viability.
   - **Use Case:** Cryptocurrencies with real-world utility, such as Ethereum or Chainlink, tend to have higher long-term value.
   - **Tokenomics:** The supply, demand, and distribution model of a cryptocurrency can significantly affect its price potential.
   - **Partnerships and Integrations:** Strategic partnerships with big companies or financial institutions can drive the adoption of a cryptocurrency, leading to price appreciation.

4. **Market Sentiment Indicators:**
   Tools like the **Fear and Greed Index** track sentiment in the market and provide insights into whether investors are feeling optimistic (greedy) or pessimistic (fearful). Sentiment indicators can be used alongside technical and fundamental analysis to gauge the overall mood of the market.

Psychology of Crypto Trading

Understanding human psychology is an important aspect of mastering market dynamics. Crypto markets are highly emotional, and investor behaviour can often be driven by fear, greed, and the herd mentality. To succeed in crypto trading, you need to develop emotional discipline and avoid falling into the following psychological traps:

1. **FOMO (Fear of Missing Out):**
   The fear of missing out on a price rally often leads investors to jump into trades without fully understanding the underlying fundamentals. FOMO is especially prevalent during bull markets when prices are rising rapidly. However, investing based on FOMO can result in buying at the top and experiencing significant losses when prices correct.
2. **Panic Selling:**
   During bear markets or periods of price decline, panic selling can lead investors to liquidate their holdings out of fear. This reaction can lock in losses and cause investors to miss out on future price recoveries.
3. **Herd Mentality:**
   The crypto market is prone to herd mentality, where large groups of investors follow the same trades, often without conducting thorough research. This can lead to market bubbles, where asset prices become overinflated, followed by sharp corrections when the bubble bursts.

To avoid these psychological pitfalls, practice emotional detachment and make decisions based on logic, not emotions. Developing a clear investment strategy, setting stop-loss orders, and regularly reviewing your portfolio will help you maintain discipline in volatile markets.

Practical Strategies for Mastering Market Dynamics

1. **Keep a Long-Term Perspective:**
   The crypto market can be incredibly volatile, with significant price swings occurring within short periods. To avoid being swayed by daily fluctuations, take a long-term approach to your investments. Focus on projects with strong fundamentals, real-world use cases, and active development communities.
2. **Follow Market Trends, Not Noise:**
   Crypto markets are often filled with hype, rumours, and speculation. It's important to distinguish between legitimate market trends and fleeting noise. Focus on data-driven analysis and trends that reflect the long-term potential of an asset.
3. **Be Prepared for Volatility:**
   Volatility is a natural part of the crypto market. Embrace it and use it to your advantage by employing strategies such as swing trading, day trading, or dollar-cost averaging. However, always ensure that you have an exit strategy in place to protect your profits and limit your losses.
4. **Diversify Your Portfolio:**
   As with any investment strategy, diversification is key to managing risk. Spread your investments across different cryptocurrencies, including large-cap coins like Bitcoin and Ethereum, as well as promising altcoins. Diversifying into different sectors, such as DeFi, NFTs, and privacy coins, can also help mitigate risk.

Conclusion

Mastering the dynamics of the crypto market requires understanding both the technical and psychological aspects that drive price movements. By staying informed, conducting thorough analysis, and managing your emotions, you can position yourself to thrive in the volatile world of cryptocurrencies. Remember that the market is always evolving.

6 Timing the Market vs. Time in the Market

Cryptocurrency is one of the most volatile asset classes, with prices often swinging dramatically within hours or even minutes. This volatility tempts many investors to try timing the market—buying low and selling high to maximize profits. However, the alternative approach, known as "time in the market," focuses on long-term holding, underpinned by the belief that market trends favour patient investors.

In this chapter, we'll compare these two strategies, explore their risks and benefits, and help you determine which approach suits your goals.

What Is Market Timing?

Market timing is an investment strategy where investors attempt to predict future price movements and make trades accordingly. The goal is to buy at the lowest price and sell at the peak, maximizing profits.

Methods Used in Market Timing:

1. **Technical Analysis:** Analyzing price charts, patterns, and indicators to predict movements.
2. **Fundamental Analysis:** Assessing a project's underlying value and market potential.
3. **Sentiment Analysis:** Gauging the mood of the market, often by monitoring social media or news trends.

While market timing can yield significant gains, it's notoriously difficult to execute consistently.

The Risks of Timing the Market

1. **Emotional Decisions:**
   Fear of missing out (FOMO) and panic selling often lead to poor timing. Emotional decisions can cause you to buy at the peak and sell at the bottom.
2. **Unpredictable Market Moves:**
   Even experienced traders struggle to predict price movements with accuracy. Unexpected news, regulations, or events can disrupt the best-laid plans.
3. **High Transaction Costs:**
   Frequent buying and selling can incur fees on exchanges, eating into profits over time.
4. **Missed Opportunities:**
   If you're out of the market during a sudden price surge, you may miss significant gains.

What Is Time in the Market?

"Time in the market" emphasizes holding investments over the long term, regardless of short-term volatility. This strategy is rooted in the belief that crypto markets, like traditional markets, tend to grow over time as adoption increases and technology matures.

The Benefits of Time in the Market

1. **Compounding Gains:**
   By staying invested, you benefit from cumulative growth over time, especially in assets like Bitcoin and Ethereum, which have demonstrated long-term upward trends.
2. **Reduced Stress:**
   Long-term holders aren't concerned with daily price fluctuations, making it easier to stay disciplined.
3. **Lower Costs:**
   Fewer trades mean lower transaction fees and tax

liabilities.
4. **Capturing Bull Markets:**
By staying in the market, you're positioned to benefit from major price surges that often happen unpredictably.

HODLing: The Crypto Approach to Time in the Market

HODLing, a misspelling of "hold," has become a popular term in the crypto community. It refers to the strategy of holding onto your assets during both bull and bear markets.

Why HODLing Works:

- Crypto markets are cyclical, with periods of extreme volatility followed by extended growth.
- Many long-term holders of Bitcoin and Ethereum, despite enduring multiple crashes, have seen massive returns over time.

Combining Both Strategies

For most investors, a hybrid approach works best. Here's how you can combine market timing with long-term holding:

1. **Core and Satellite Portfolio:**
    - Dedicate the majority of your portfolio to long-term holdings (core).
    - Use a smaller portion for short-term trading opportunities (satellite).
2. **Dollar-Cost Averaging (DCA):**
    - Invest a fixed amount at regular intervals, regardless of the market price.
    - This reduces the risk of buying at the peak and smooths out the impact of volatility.
3. **Set Clear Goals:**
    - Use market timing to capitalize on specific opportunities (e.g., a project launch or event).

    - Hold core assets for long-term value creation.
4. **Take Partial Profits:**
    - When an asset performs well, consider selling a portion to lock in profits while retaining some for future growth.

Case Study: Bitcoin

Let's compare two hypothetical investors:

- **Investor A** tries to time the market by buying Bitcoin at $10,000 and selling at $12,000, only to see the price rise to $60,000 later.
- **Investor B** buys Bitcoin at $10,000 and holds it through bull and bear markets, ultimately reaping the rewards of the long-term uptrend.

Investor B's patience and belief in the asset yield significantly higher returns, despite the short-term volatility endured along the way.

Strategies to Avoid Common Pitfalls

1. **Avoid Over-Trading:**
   Excessive trading can lead to losses, especially when fees and taxes are factored in.
2. **Stick to Your Plan:**
   Whether you're a trader or a holder, having a clear strategy helps you avoid impulsive decisions.
3. **Beware of Influencers:**
   Social media is rife with hype and speculation. Trust your research over market chatter.
4. **Diversify Your Timing:**
   If you're trading, stagger your buys and sells to avoid the risk of making a single poorly timed decision.

Conclusion

Timing the market can be lucrative but requires skill, discipline, and the ability to manage risks effectively. On the other hand, long-term holding, or time in the market, offers a simpler and often more reliable path to wealth creation in crypto.

For most investors, a balanced approach that combines the two strategies is the most practical. By staying informed, disciplined, and patient, you can navigate the volatile crypto market with confidence.

7 Identifying High-Potential Crypto Projects

The cryptocurrency market is teeming with opportunities—but not all projects are created equal. Some tokens offer groundbreaking technology and real-world applications, while others are speculative ventures or outright scams. Identifying high-potential crypto projects is essential for building a successful portfolio.

In this chapter, we'll explore the key factors to evaluate when assessing a cryptocurrency project, the red flags to watch out for, and how to conduct thorough research before investing.

The Fundamentals of a Crypto Project

Before investing in any cryptocurrency, it's crucial to understand the project's foundation. Here are the main elements to evaluate:

1. **The Whitepaper**
    - A crypto project's whitepaper is its blueprint, outlining its purpose, technology, and use case.
    - **Key Questions to Answer:**
        - What problem does the project aim to solve?
        - How does the technology work?
        - Is the goal achievable, or does it sound overly ambitious?

2. **The Team**
    - A project's success often hinges on the quality and expertise of its team.
    - **Things to Research:**
        - Do team members have relevant experience in blockchain, tech, or finance?
        - Are they transparent about their identities and backgrounds?
        - Have they been involved in successful projects before?

3. **The Roadmap**
    - A clear, realistic roadmap shows the project's long-term vision and how it plans to achieve its goals.
    - **Look For:**
        - Detailed timelines for development milestones.
        - Achievements that align with the roadmap.
        - Regular updates and progress reports.

The Technology Behind the Project

Understanding the technology is crucial for determining whether a project has long-term potential:

1. **Consensus Mechanism**
    - How does the network achieve consensus? Common mechanisms include Proof of Work

(PoW), Proof of Stake (PoS), and newer models like Delegated Proof of Stake (DPoS) or Proof of Authority (PoA).
- Consider energy efficiency, scalability, and security.

2. **Scalability**
    - Can the blockchain handle high transaction volumes without sacrificing speed or security?
    - Projects like Solana and Polygon focus on scalability, making them attractive for future growth.

3. **Interoperability**
    - Can the project integrate or communicate with other blockchains?
    - Interoperable blockchains like Polkadot and Cosmos are designed to connect disparate networks.

4. **Smart Contract Capabilities**
    - Does the project support smart contracts? Platforms like Ethereum, Cardano, and Binance Smart Chain enable decentralized applications (dApps), adding utility to the blockchain.

Tokenomics: The Economics of the Token

Tokenomics refers to the economic model of a cryptocurrency. A well-designed token economy is essential for sustainable growth:

1. **Supply and Demand**
    - Total Supply: Is the total token supply capped, or can more be minted? A limited supply (like Bitcoin's 21 million cap) often drives value.
    - Demand Drivers: What incentivizes users to hold or use the token?
2. **Distribution**
    - How are the tokens distributed? Excessive allocation to insiders or developers can signal centralization or potential market manipulation.
3. **Utility**
    - What is the token used for? Projects with clear use cases (e.g., governance, transaction fees, staking) are more likely to succeed.
4. **Inflation or Deflation**
    - Does the token have mechanisms to control inflation or incentivize holding? Examples include burning tokens to reduce supply or staking rewards for holders.

Community and Adoption

A strong, engaged community is often a good indicator of a project's potential:

1. **Community Size and Engagement**
   - Platforms like Reddit, Twitter, and Discord can provide insight into community sentiment.
   - Look for active discussions and genuine interest rather than bots or paid promotions.
2. **Partnerships and Integrations**
   - Does the project have credible partnerships with businesses or institutions?
   - Integrations with existing ecosystems can boost adoption.
3. **Real-World Use Cases**
   - Projects that solve real-world problems or improve existing systems tend to have more staying power.

Red Flags to Avoid

While some projects show promise, others may be scams or poorly conceived ventures. Watch out for these red flags:

1. **Unrealistic Promises**
   - Be wary of projects promising guaranteed returns or outrageous growth rates.
2. **Lack of Transparency**
   - Anonymous teams or vague whitepapers are major warning signs.
3. **High Token Allocation to Insiders**

- Projects where a large percentage of tokens are held by founders or developers can lead to market manipulation.

4. **Overemphasis on Marketing**
    - Excessive hype without substance often indicates a lack of long-term viability.

5. **Unverified Claims**
    - If a project claims partnerships or achievements, verify these claims through credible sources.

Conducting Thorough Research

To identify high-potential projects, dedicate time to research:

1. **Use Reliable Sources**
    - Explore reputable crypto news platforms like CoinDesk, CoinTelegraph, and Messari.

2. **Follow Developers and Teams**
    - Developers often share updates and insights on platforms like Twitter and GitHub.

3. **Analyze On-Chain Data**
    - Tools like Glassnode, Etherscan, and Nansen can provide insights into wallet activity, transaction volume, and network health.

4. **Join Communities**
   - Engage with communities on Telegram, Discord, or Reddit to get firsthand insights into project developments and sentiment.

5. **Test the Technology**
   - If possible, use the platform or dApp yourself to understand its usability and functionality.

Case Study: Ethereum

Ethereum is a prime example of a high-potential project that has stood the test of time:

- **Whitepaper:** Clearly outlined its vision for smart contracts and decentralized applications.
- **Technology:** Introduced a groundbreaking platform for programmable blockchains.
- **Community:** Fostered one of the largest and most active developer ecosystems.
- **Adoption:** Enabled thousands of projects, including DeFi and NFTs, to thrive on its platform.

By focusing on these factors, early investors in Ethereum were able to recognize its long-term potential.

Conclusion

Identifying high-potential crypto projects requires diligence, research, and a healthy dose of skepticism. By analyzing the fundamentals, technology, tokenomics, and community behind a project, you can make informed decisions and avoid costly mistakes.

8 The Psychology of Crypto Investing

Investing in cryptocurrency is as much about mindset as it is about strategy. The volatile and unpredictable nature of the market can evoke strong emotions like fear, greed, and doubt, often leading to impulsive decisions. Developing the right psychological approach is crucial for navigating the highs and lows of crypto investing.

In this chapter, we'll explore the emotional challenges of investing in crypto, common psychological traps, and practical strategies to cultivate a mindset for success.

Emotions in Crypto Investing

Cryptocurrency markets operate 24/7 and are highly susceptible to news and sentiment, making emotional control a constant challenge.

1. **Fear of Missing Out (FOMO):**
    - FOMO occurs when investors see others making profits and rush to buy into a rising market, often at the peak.
    - Example: Buying a token during a sudden price surge, only to watch it crash shortly after.
2. **Fear, Uncertainty, and Doubt (FUD):**
    - Negative news or rumors can trigger panic selling, even when the fundamentals of a project remain strong.
    - Example: Selling during a market dip due to unfounded regulatory fears.
3. **Greed:**
    - Greed can lead to overtrading, ignoring risk, or holding onto an asset too long in hopes of even greater gains.
    - Example: Not taking profits during a bull market, only to see your portfolio lose value in a correction.

4. **Impatience:**
   - Crypto investors often expect quick returns and may abandon promising projects if they don't see immediate results.
5. **Overconfidence:**
   - Success in one trade can lead to overconfidence, causing investors to take unnecessary risks without thorough research.

Common Psychological Traps

1. **Herd Mentality:**
   - Following the crowd without doing your own research can lead to poor decisions. The crowd is often wrong, especially during bubbles or crashes.
2. **Recency Bias:**
   - Believing that recent price trends will continue indefinitely, whether bullish or bearish.
   - Example: Assuming a token will keep rising just because it has been trending upward for weeks.
3. **Loss Aversion:**
   - The pain of losing money often outweighs the joy of gaining it. This can lead to holding onto losing positions too long or selling winners too early.
4. **Confirmation Bias:**
   - Seeking out information that supports your existing beliefs while ignoring evidence to the contrary.
   - Example: Only reading positive news about a token you own and ignoring red flags.

Developing a Winning Mindset

1. **Have a Plan:**
   - Create a clear investment strategy that includes

entry and exit points, risk tolerance, and long-term goals. Stick to your plan, even during market turbulence.
2. **Manage Expectations:**
   - Accept that crypto is highly volatile and that losses are part of the journey. Focus on long-term growth rather than short-term gains.
3. **Practice Emotional Discipline:**
   - Avoid making decisions based on emotions. Use data, research, and logic to guide your actions.
4. **Stay Informed but Detached:**
   - Keep up with market trends and news, but don't let them dictate your every move. Develop the ability to separate noise from valuable insights.
5. **Focus on What You Can Control:**
   - You can't control market movements, but you can control how you react to them. Stay calm, patient, and disciplined.

Strategies for Overcoming Emotional Challenges

1. **Set Stop-Loss and Take-Profit Levels:**
   - Use stop-loss orders to minimize losses and take-profit orders to lock in gains automatically.
2. **Dollar-Cost Averaging (DCA):**
   - Regularly invest a fixed amount, regardless of market conditions. This removes the stress of timing the market perfectly.
3. **Diversify Your Portfolio:**
   - Diversification reduces the emotional impact of a single asset's performance.
4. **Limit Your Exposure:**
   - Only invest money you can afford to lose. Knowing that your financial stability isn't at risk will help you stay rational.

5. **Take Breaks:**
    - Constantly monitoring the market can lead to burnout and impulsive decisions. Step away when needed to maintain perspective.

Case Study: Bitcoin's 2017 Bull Run

During the 2017 bull run, Bitcoin reached an all-time high of nearly $20,000. Many new investors entered the market, driven by FOMO. When the market crashed in early 2018, panic selling led to significant losses for those who hadn't planned for volatility.

Investors who maintained emotional discipline and held onto their Bitcoin during the subsequent bear market saw it recover and surpass $60,000 in later years. This highlights the importance of patience and long-term thinking.

Mindfulness and Crypto Investing

Practicing mindfulness can help you stay calm and focused in a chaotic market:

- **Meditation:** Spend a few minutes each day practicing mindfulness meditation to improve emotional control.
- **Journaling:** Keep a journal of your investment decisions and the emotions behind them. Reflecting on past actions can help you identify patterns and improve.
- **Perspective:** Remember that crypto is just one part of your life. Keeping a balanced perspective reduces stress and impulsive behaviour.

The Role of Education

Knowledge is your best defence against emotional decision-making:

- Learn the basics of blockchain technology, trading, and market analysis.
- Stay updated on industry developments through reputable sources.
- Join communities of experienced investors who can provide guidance and support.

Conclusion

The psychological challenges of crypto investing are significant, but they can be managed with the right mindset and strategies. By staying disciplined, focusing on your goals, and controlling your emotions, you can make more rational decisions and increase your chances of long-term success.

9 Crypto Trading Strategies

Trading cryptocurrency is a dynamic and potentially profitable activity, but it comes with high risk. The ability to capitalize on market movements while managing risk is the hallmark of a skilled trader. In this chapter, we'll explore different trading strategies, when to use them, and how to refine your approach to maximize profitability while minimizing losses.

Types of Crypto Trading

Before we dive into specific strategies, it's essential to understand the different types of crypto trading:

1. **Day Trading**
   - Day trading involves buying and selling crypto assets within the same day, capitalizing on short-term price fluctuations.
   - Day traders typically make multiple trades per day and rely on technical analysis to make quick decisions.
2. **Swing Trading**
   - Swing trading involves holding assets for several days or weeks to capitalize on short- to medium-term price movements.
   - Traders use both technical and fundamental analysis to predict market trends and make informed decisions.
3. **Scalping**
   - Scalping is an ultra-short-term strategy where traders make dozens or hundreds of trades throughout the day to capture small price movements.
   - This strategy requires significant time, focus, and market liquidity.
4. **Position Trading**
   - Position trading focuses on long-term gains by holding assets for months or years.
   - Position traders typically rely on fundamental analysis, choosing assets with strong long-term growth

potential.
5. **Arbitrage**
    - Arbitrage is a strategy where traders exploit price differences for the same asset on different exchanges.
    - Traders buy low on one exchange and sell high on another, making a profit from the discrepancy.

The Role of Technical Analysis

Crypto trading often relies heavily on technical analysis (TA), which uses historical price data, chart patterns, and technical indicators to predict future price movements. Here are some of the most common tools used in TA:

1. **Candlestick Charts**
    - Candlestick charts display price movements over a specific period and show open, high, low, and close prices. They help traders identify trends, reversals, and potential entry and exit points.
2. **Support and Resistance Levels**
    - Support is a price level where an asset tends to find buying interest, preventing further declines.
    - Resistance is a level where selling pressure is strong enough to prevent the price from rising further.
    - Identifying these levels helps traders make better entry and exit decisions.
3. **Moving Averages (MA)**
    - Moving averages smooth out price data to identify trends. The most common are the Simple Moving Average (SMA) and the Exponential Moving Average (EMA).
    - The 50-day and 200-day moving averages are key levels to watch for potential buy or sell signals.
4. **Relative Strength Index (RSI)**
    - RSI measures the speed and change of price movements, indicating overbought or oversold conditions. A value above 70 suggests an asset is overbought, while below 30 indicates it is oversold.

5. **MACD (Moving Average Convergence Divergence)**
    - MACD is a momentum indicator that shows the relationship between two moving averages (usually the 12-day EMA and the 26-day EMA).
    - Traders watch for MACD crossovers as potential buy or sell signals.

Common Crypto Trading Strategies

1. **Trend Following**
    - The core principle of trend following is to "buy high, sell higher" or "sell low, buy lower."
    - Traders use indicators like moving averages and trendlines to identify upward or downward trends and make trades in the direction of the trend.
2. **Breakout Trading**
    - Breakout traders look for a price to break out of a support or resistance level. A breakout signifies that the price is likely to continue in the direction of the break, presenting a trading opportunity.
    - Traders typically use volume indicators to confirm the strength of a breakout.
3. **Range Trading**
    - Range trading involves buying at support and selling at resistance within a defined range. This strategy works best in markets without a strong trend, where prices oscillate between predictable support and resistance levels.
    - Traders use oscillators like RSI or Stochastic Oscillator to help identify overbought or oversold conditions, signalling potential buying or selling opportunities.
4. **News-Based Trading**
    - This strategy involves trading based on news or events that can cause significant price fluctuations, such as government regulations, partnerships, technological updates, or market sentiment shifts.
    - Crypto news traders need to be fast and responsive, as prices often react quickly to news. Keeping up with

trusted news sources and social media platforms is essential for success in this strategy.
5. **Mean Reversion**
    - The mean reversion strategy is based on the assumption that prices will eventually return to their average or "mean."
    - When prices move too far above or below the mean (often determined by a moving average), traders take a contrarian position, betting that prices will revert to the mean.

Risk Management in Crypto Trading

Given the volatility of the crypto market, risk management is crucial for long-term success. Here are some key risk management techniques:

1. **Position Sizing**
    - Determine how much of your portfolio to allocate to each trade. This helps you limit losses if the market moves against you.
    - A common approach is the "1% Rule," which suggests risking no more than 1% of your capital on any single trade.

2. **Stop-Loss Orders**
    - A stop-loss is an order placed to automatically sell an asset if its price drops to a certain level, limiting your losses.
    - Set stop-loss orders based on technical analysis, ensuring they are far enough away to avoid being triggered by normal price fluctuations but close enough to protect your portfolio.

3. **Take-Profit Orders**
    - A take-profit order automatically sells an asset when its price hits a predetermined level of profit.
    - This ensures that you lock in gains without needing to

monitor the market constantly.

4. **Risk-to-Reward Ratio**
    o Assess the risk of each trade relative to the potential reward. A common risk-to-reward ratio for crypto traders is 1:3, meaning you aim to make three times as much as you are willing to risk.
    o For example, if you're risking $100, your target profit should be $300.

5. **Diversification**
    o Avoid putting all your capital into one asset. Diversifying across different cryptocurrencies reduces the impact of a single asset's volatility on your portfolio.

Using Leverage in Crypto Trading

Leverage allows traders to control a larger position with a smaller amount of capital, amplifying both potential profits and losses. While leverage can be enticing, it's important to use it cautiously:

1. **Understand the Risks:**
    o With high leverage, small market movements can result in significant losses. Ensure you understand how leverage works before using it.
2. **Use Leverage Sparingly:**
    o Only use leverage when you have a clear understanding of the market direction and when your risk management plan is in place.
3. **Set Stop-Loss Orders:**
    o When using leverage, setting stop-loss orders is crucial to protecting your capital.

Psychology of Trading: Avoiding Emotional Traps

Crypto trading can be stressful, especially during periods of high volatility. To succeed, you need to control your emotions:

1. **Stick to Your Plan:**
    - Follow your trading strategy and avoid reacting to market noise or FOMO.
2. **Accept Losses as Part of the Process:**
    - Every trader experiences losses. Accept them as part of the learning process and don't let them derail your strategy.
3. **Don't Chase the Market:**
    - Avoid chasing after a "hot" trade. Stick to your strategy and wait for favourable conditions rather than jumping into trades out of impatience.

Conclusion

Crypto trading is a rewarding but high-risk endeavour that requires skill, discipline, and a well-defined strategy. By mastering technical analysis, understanding various trading strategies, and implementing strong risk management practices, you can navigate the volatility and achieve long-term success.

10 Securing Your Crypto Assets

As the popularity of cryptocurrency grows, so does the risk of theft, hacking, and fraud. With billions of dollars invested in digital assets, crypto investors face significant security threats, ranging from cyber-attacks to scams. Ensuring that your crypto assets are secure is crucial for long-term success in the market. In this chapter, we'll explore the best practices for protecting your digital assets and securing your investment.

Understanding Crypto Security Risks

Crypto assets are inherently different from traditional investments in that they are decentralized and stored digitally. This offers many advantages but also presents unique security challenges:

1. **Hacking:**
    - Crypto exchanges and wallets are prime targets for hackers. In 2021 alone, over $14 billion worth of crypto was stolen through hacks.
    - Hackers can gain access to private keys, allowing them to steal assets from your wallet or exchange account.

2. **Phishing Scams:**
    - Phishing is a technique used by scammers to trick you into revealing private information such as your wallet's private key, seed phrase, or exchange login credentials.

- This is often done through fake websites, emails, or messages that look like they come from a trusted source.

3. **Rug Pulls and Ponzi Schemes:**
    - Fraudulent projects may promise high returns and then disappear with investors' funds. These scams, often referred to as "rug pulls," can happen in both new and established markets.

4. **Lack of Regulation:**
    - The decentralized nature of crypto means that there are fewer protections in place compared to traditional financial systems. Investors may find it difficult to recover stolen funds due to the lack of regulation and oversight.

5. **Physical Theft:**
    - If your private keys or seed phrase are stored improperly (such as on paper or an unencrypted digital file), they are at risk of being physically stolen.

Best Practices for Securing Your Crypto Assets

To safeguard your crypto assets, you must adopt a multi-layered approach to security. Here are the key practices to follow:

1. **Use Hardware Wallets (Cold Storage):**
    - Hardware wallets are physical devices that store your private keys offline, making them significantly more secure from hacking attempts. Popular options include Ledger and Trezor.
    - By keeping your assets in cold storage, you ensure that they are not exposed to online threats such as hacking or phishing.

2. **Enable Two-Factor Authentication (2FA):**
    - Always enable 2FA on exchanges and wallets to add an extra layer of protection.
    - 2FA requires not only your password but also a second form of verification, such as a code sent to your phone or generated by an authenticator app like Google Authenticator.
    - Never rely on SMS-based 2FA, as it can be intercepted through SIM swapping attacks. Instead, use app-based 2FA whenever possible.

3. **Use Strong, Unique Passwords:**
    - Create complex passwords that include a combination of letters, numbers, and special characters.
    - Avoid using easily guessable information such as birthdays, names, or common phrases.
    - Use a password manager to keep track of your passwords securely, especially if you manage

multiple accounts.

4. **Backup Your Private Keys and Seed Phrases:**
    - Backup your private keys and seed phrases in multiple secure locations (such as a safe deposit box or encrypted USB drive).
    - Never store your backup in online storage or unprotected locations, as they could be compromised.
    - If you lose access to your private keys or seed phrase, you lose access to your crypto assets permanently.

5. **Be Cautious with Phishing Attempts:**
    - Be vigilant when clicking on links in emails, text messages, or social media. Always verify that the URL is correct before entering any personal information.
    - Double-check the legitimacy of any communication asking for sensitive information, especially if the sender is offering something that seems too good to be true.
    - When in doubt, always visit the official website of the crypto exchange or wallet provider directly rather than clicking on a link in an email or message.

6. **Avoid Public Wi-Fi for Crypto Transactions:**
    - Public Wi-Fi networks are not secure and can be

exploited by hackers to intercept your communication or steal your login credentials.

- When accessing your crypto accounts or making transactions, always use a private and secure internet connection, ideally with a VPN (Virtual Private Network) for added protection.

7. **Keep Software and Devices Up to Date:**

    - Regularly update your computer, mobile devices, and wallets to ensure they have the latest security patches.
    - This reduces the likelihood of your system being compromised by known vulnerabilities.

8. **Limit Exposure on Exchanges:**

    - While exchanges provide convenience, they are also prime targets for hackers.
    - Only keep the amount of crypto on exchanges that you plan to trade or use in the short term.
    - Transfer your assets to a hardware wallet or other secure storage when not actively trading.

9. **Monitor Your Accounts and Transactions:**

    - Regularly check your crypto wallets and exchange accounts for any unauthorized activity.
    - Use block explorers to track transactions and ensure that no one has accessed your funds without your knowledge.

Decentralized Finance (DeFi) and Security

DeFi platforms allow users to engage in financial activities without intermediaries like banks, but they come with specific security risks:

1. **Smart Contract Vulnerabilities:**

    - DeFi protocols are based on smart contracts, which are susceptible to bugs or vulnerabilities.
    - Conduct research to ensure the smart contract has been audited by a reputable third party before using the platform.

2. **Beware of Yield Farming and Liquidity Pools:**

    - Some DeFi projects promise high returns through yield farming or providing liquidity to decentralized exchanges (DEXs). While these can be profitable, they also carry risks such as impermanent loss or project failures.
    - Ensure that you fully understand the risks before participating in these activities.

3. **Decentralized Exchange (DEX) Risks:**

    - While DEXs provide privacy and control over your funds, they can be more susceptible to scams or attacks.
    - Be cautious when interacting with lesser-known DEXs and always verify their security and

reputation.

Protecting Your Crypto from Rug Pulls and Scams

While securing your assets against technical vulnerabilities is essential, it's also important to protect yourself from scams and fraudulent projects:

1. **Conduct Thorough Research on Projects:**
    - Always research any project before investing, especially newer coins or tokens. Check the team's background, whitepaper, and community engagement.
    - Look for signs of legitimacy, such as audits by reputable firms or partnerships with established entities.

2. **Avoid "Too Good to Be True" Promises:**
    - High returns with little risk are often a sign of a scam. If an investment opportunity seems too good to be true, it likely is.
    - Be cautious of projects with unclear use cases, anonymous teams, or promises of guaranteed profits.

3. **Check for a Community and Active Development:**
    - Legitimate projects usually have an active community and regular updates from the development team.

- Scams often have weak or no community engagement and minimal updates from developers.

Case Study: The Mt. Gox Hack

One of the most infamous examples of crypto theft occurred with the Mt. Gox exchange in 2014. At its peak, Mt. Gox handled over 70% of global Bitcoin transactions. However, hackers exploited security vulnerabilities, leading to the theft of 850,000 BTC (worth billions at the time). This incident demonstrated the importance of securing your assets and using trusted exchanges. The majority of victims lost their assets because they didn't take proper precautions, leaving them vulnerable to hacks.

Conclusion

Securing your crypto assets is critical to safeguarding your investment. By following best practices such as using hardware wallets, enabling two-factor authentication, being cautious of phishing attacks, and practicing proper risk management, you can protect your digital wealth from threats. Crypto may be decentralized, but security is still your responsibility.

11 Maximizing Long-Term Growth in Crypto Investments

Cryptocurrency can be a powerful tool for wealth accumulation, but to maximize the long-term growth of your portfolio, a strategic, patient approach is essential. Many investors are drawn to the volatility of crypto markets for short-term gains, but those who understand how to leverage the market for long-term wealth-building will likely come out ahead. In this chapter, we'll explore how to structure your crypto portfolio, the importance of diversification, and strategies for ensuring your investments grow steadily over time.

The Importance of Long-Term Thinking

While crypto markets are known for their volatility, history has shown that patience and long-term strategies tend to yield better returns for investors who can withstand market fluctuations. Key to long-term success is the understanding that crypto is a rapidly evolving sector, and price fluctuations should be viewed in the context of the long-term trajectory rather than short-term noise.

Why Long-Term Thinking Pays Off

- **Technological Growth:** Cryptocurrencies and blockchain technology are continuously evolving. By holding assets in established, high-potential projects, you can benefit from technological advancements and adoption.

- **Accumulating Wealth:** While volatility may present opportunities for quick profits, the most successful crypto investors often hold their assets for years, allowing them to appreciate substantially as the market matures.

- **Hedging Against Inflation:** Many investors view Bitcoin and other cryptocurrencies as a hedge against traditional fiat inflation. As more people adopt crypto as an alternative investment, the value of digital assets may continue to rise over the long term.

Building a Crypto Portfolio for the Long-Term

The key to long-term crypto growth lies in diversifying your investments across a range of different assets. A well-balanced portfolio can withstand market swings and capitalize on different opportunities as they arise. Here's how to approach portfolio construction:

1. **Focus on Established Assets**
   While it's tempting to chase after new coins that promise high returns, the most successful long-term portfolios tend to be built around established, reliable assets. For example:

   - **Bitcoin (BTC):** Often called "digital gold," Bitcoin has remained the flagship crypto asset due to its proven track record and widespread adoption.

   - **Ethereum (ETH):** Ethereum's ability to support smart contracts and decentralized applications makes it a cornerstone of the crypto space.

   - **Other Top Altcoins:** Assets like Binance Coin (BNB), Cardano (ADA), and Solana (SOL) offer strong

growth potential and utility within the ecosystem.

2. **Allocate Funds to High-Potential Projects**
   While Bitcoin and Ethereum are likely to remain dominant, many altcoins have the potential for significant growth as the market matures. Look for projects with strong use cases, solid development teams, and real-world adoption. These could include:

   - **Decentralized Finance (DeFi) Tokens:** Platforms like Uniswap (UNI), Aave (AAVE), and Compound (COMP) are gaining traction in the DeFi space, where decentralized financial services are growing in popularity.

   - **Layer-2 Solutions:** Layer-2 scaling solutions like Polygon (MATIC) offer scalability to popular blockchain networks, providing the infrastructure needed for the mass adoption of crypto applications.

3. **Consider Stablecoins for Stability**
   In a highly volatile market, stablecoins like Tether (USDT) or USD Coin (USDC) can provide stability. These digital assets are pegged to traditional currencies like the U.S. dollar, reducing exposure to price swings. Stablecoins can also serve as a safe haven during market downturns or a useful tool for yield farming.

4. **Long-Term Staking and Yield Farming**
   Many crypto assets offer rewards through staking or yield farming, where you earn passive income by locking your assets into the network. Staking involves participating in a proof-of-stake consensus mechanism to help secure a

blockchain network, while yield farming allows you to earn interest by providing liquidity to decentralized protocols. These strategies allow you to compound your returns over time.

- **Staking:** Popular staking coins include Ethereum (after its transition to proof-of-stake), Cardano (ADA), and Polkadot (DOT).

- **Yield Farming:** You can earn returns by providing liquidity to decentralized exchanges like Uniswap or lending platforms like Aave or Compound.

Dollar-Cost Averaging (DCA)

One of the most effective strategies for long-term growth in any volatile market, including crypto, is dollar-cost averaging (DCA). DCA involves investing a fixed amount of money at regular intervals (e.g., weekly or monthly), regardless of market conditions. This strategy smooths out the impact of market volatility, ensuring you don't invest too heavily at a market peak or miss out during a market dip.

Why DCA Works in Crypto:

- **Reduced Impact of Timing Risk:** Crypto markets are notoriously volatile, and trying to time the market perfectly can lead to missed opportunities. DCA removes the pressure of making perfect timing decisions.

- **Consistency:** By sticking to a regular investment schedule, you maintain consistency in your approach and reduce the emotional stress of watching daily price fluctuations.

- **More Units for Lower Prices:** During market dips, you buy more units of your chosen asset for the same dollar amount, allowing you to accumulate more over time.

Taking Advantage of Crypto-Related Financial Products

As the crypto ecosystem matures, traditional financial institutions and blockchain-specific companies are offering innovative ways for investors to grow their wealth. Here are some ways you can take advantage of these opportunities:

1. **Crypto Index Funds and ETFs**
   Crypto index funds and exchange-traded funds (ETFs) are designed to give investors exposure to a diverse basket of cryptocurrencies. These products allow you to invest in a broad selection of assets without having to pick individual coins yourself. Popular funds and ETFs include:

   - **Grayscale Bitcoin Trust (GBTC):** A trust that holds Bitcoin, allowing you to gain exposure to the asset through traditional financial markets.

   - **Bitwise 10 Crypto Index Fund (BITW):** This fund tracks the performance of the top 10 cryptocurrencies, providing diversified exposure to the market.

2. **Crypto Lending Platforms**
   Lending platforms like BlockFi, Celsius, and Nexo allow you to earn interest on your crypto holdings by lending them out to borrowers. These platforms offer an easy way to generate passive income and increase the value of your

assets without having to sell them.

Adapting to the Evolution of Crypto Technology

Cryptocurrency and blockchain technology are rapidly evolving, and staying informed is key to ensuring your portfolio stays ahead of the curve. Here's how to keep up with the evolving landscape:

1. **Stay Informed About Blockchain Advancements**
   Constant innovation in blockchain technology presents new opportunities. Keep an eye on emerging technologies like:

   - **NFTs (Non-Fungible Tokens):** These digital assets represent ownership of unique items like art, collectibles, or intellectual property. While they're still relatively new, they have significant potential for growth.

   - **Layer-2 Solutions:** These protocols are built on top of existing blockchains to improve scalability, transaction speed, and reduce fees.

2. **Participate in Governance and Community Initiatives**
   Many blockchain projects give token holders the opportunity to participate in governance, where you can vote on the future direction of the project. By holding governance tokens, you not only benefit from potential value appreciation but also gain insight into the future of the project.

Risk Management for Long-Term Crypto Growth

While long-term growth is the goal, it's essential to implement effective risk management strategies to ensure that your portfolio withstands downturns and remains protected from major losses. Here are some steps to manage risk:

1. **Set Realistic Expectations**
   The crypto market is volatile, so it's important to set realistic expectations for your returns. While substantial profits are possible, significant losses can also occur. Ensure that you are prepared for both scenarios.

2. **Regular Portfolio Rebalancing**
   Periodically review and rebalance your portfolio to ensure it aligns with your long-term goals. As markets evolve, some assets may outperform others, requiring you to adjust your allocations. Rebalancing allows you to lock in profits from high-performing assets and reallocate funds to emerging opportunities.

3. **Protect Against Downside Risk**
   Consider using stop-loss orders or setting target exit points to protect your investments in case of significant downturns. These tools help ensure that you don't suffer massive losses during a market correction.

Conclusion

Maximizing long-term growth in crypto investments requires a thoughtful approach, patience, and a clear strategy. By building a diversified portfolio, using strategies like dollar-cost averaging, and staying informed about technological developments, you can grow your wealth while managing risks effectively. The crypto market offers vast opportunities, but only those who take the time to understand the space and plan for the long term will be able to capitalize on its full potential.

12 Navigating the Tax Implications of Crypto Investments

As cryptocurrency continues to grow in popularity and adoption, it brings with it a new set of tax considerations for investors. Taxation in the crypto space can be complex due to the unique nature of digital assets. The tax laws surrounding cryptocurrencies vary by country and can be subject to frequent changes as governments catch up with this rapidly evolving market. Understanding how your crypto investments are taxed is crucial for both compliance and for optimizing your financial outcomes. In this chapter, we'll explore the tax implications of crypto investing, how to properly report your crypto transactions, and strategies for managing your crypto tax liability.

Understanding Crypto Taxation

Most countries treat cryptocurrencies as taxable assets, classifying them as property or capital assets rather than currency. This classification affects how your crypto transactions are taxed, including buying, selling, trading, and even using crypto to purchase goods or services.

1. **Capital Gains Tax:**
    - **Capital Gains:** In most countries, the sale of crypto is subject to capital gains tax. If you sell an asset for a profit, the difference between your purchase price (the "basis") and the sale price is taxed as a capital gain.

- **Short-Term vs. Long-Term Capital Gains:** The tax rate for your capital gains can differ depending on how long you held the asset. In many jurisdictions, if you hold the asset for over a year, you may qualify for long-term capital gains treatment, which is often taxed at a lower rate. Short-term gains (on assets held for less than a year) are usually taxed at a higher, ordinary income tax rate.

2. **Income Tax on Mining or Staking Rewards:**

    - **Mining:** If you mine cryptocurrency, the IRS in the U.S. and other tax authorities in different countries treat the rewards as taxable income. The value of the crypto when it's mined is considered income and taxed at ordinary income rates. If you later sell the mined crypto for a profit, that gain will be subject to capital gains tax.

    - **Staking:** Similar to mining, staking rewards are often treated as income, taxed at ordinary income rates when they are earned. When you sell or exchange the staked crypto, you will then owe capital gains tax on any appreciation.

3. **Tax on Airdrops and Forks:**

    - **Airdrops:** If you receive free crypto through an airdrop (for example, tokens distributed to holders of a specific cryptocurrency), these are typically treated as income, taxable at the market value on the date you receive them.

    - **Forks:** In the case of a blockchain fork that results

in new tokens being issued to holders of the original coin, the IRS and other tax authorities may consider the value of the new tokens as income at the time they're received.

4. **Using Crypto to Pay for Goods and Services:**

    o **Taxable Event:** When you use cryptocurrency to buy goods or services, this is considered a taxable event. In many jurisdictions, such as the U.S., any profit made from the increase in value of your crypto from the time you acquired it to the time of the transaction is subject to capital gains tax.

    o **Record-Keeping:** You need to keep detailed records of any crypto transactions in which you used your holdings to make purchases. The taxable event is the difference between your purchase price and the value of the crypto at the time of the transaction.

Tracking and Reporting Crypto Transactions

Keeping track of your crypto transactions and accurately reporting them is essential to ensure compliance with tax laws. Unlike traditional financial assets, crypto transactions can be numerous and complex. Here's how to stay organized and report your crypto activity:

1. **Track All Transactions:**
    It is crucial to keep detailed records of every crypto transaction you make. This includes buying, selling,

trading, transferring, or using crypto to pay for goods or services.

- **Transaction Details to Track:** The date of the transaction, the amount of crypto involved, the value in fiat currency at the time, and any transaction fees.

- **Using Crypto Tax Software:** There are several tools and software programs that can help you track your crypto transactions automatically and generate tax reports. Examples include CoinTracker, TaxBit, and Koinly. These platforms integrate with your exchange accounts and wallets, tracking your gains and losses, and generating reports that comply with tax laws.

2. **Calculate Capital Gains and Losses:**
For every sale or trade of crypto, you need to calculate the capital gain or loss. The formula is as follows:

    - **Capital Gain = Sale Price - Purchase Price (Basis)**

    - **Capital Loss = Purchase Price (Basis) - Sale Price**
    The net capital gains (or losses) are calculated for the entire year and reported on your tax return. If you have net capital losses, these can often be used to offset other taxable income.

3. **Report Your Crypto Income:**
If you earned crypto through mining, staking, airdrops, or any other form of income, it must be reported as part of your earnings. Depending on the amount and frequency of your crypto income, it may be reported as self-

employment income or as miscellaneous income.

- **Income From Mining:** If you mined crypto, the value of the crypto on the date it was received will be taxed as income.
- **Staking Rewards:** Similar to mining, staking rewards are taxed as ordinary income.

4. **International Tax Reporting:**
   If you are a resident of a country that has cryptocurrency tax laws, but you trade on foreign exchanges, you must report all your transactions—regardless of where they took place. Some countries require additional reporting if you hold a certain amount of foreign assets, including crypto. Always check with a tax professional who understands international tax laws if you are trading across borders.

Tax Strategies for Minimizing Liability

While paying taxes on crypto is unavoidable, there are strategies that can help reduce your tax liability legally:

1. **Tax-Loss Harvesting:**
   Tax-loss harvesting is the strategy of selling assets at a loss to offset taxable gains from other investments. If you've experienced a loss on some of your crypto holdings, you can sell them to offset capital gains you may have made from other assets.

   - This strategy can help reduce your overall tax burden.

- After selling, you can repurchase the same or similar assets if you still believe in their long-term potential.

2. **Holding for the Long-Term:**
If you hold your crypto for more than one year, you may qualify for long-term capital gains tax rates, which tend to be lower than short-term rates.

    - By adopting a long-term investment strategy, you may reduce your tax rate on capital gains and improve your overall tax efficiency.

3. **Gift or Inheritance Strategies:**

    - **Gifting Crypto:** If you plan to gift crypto to family or friends, you can do so without triggering capital gains taxes, but the recipient may have to pay taxes on the crypto when they sell it.

    - **Crypto Inheritance:** In some jurisdictions, inherited crypto assets may be treated differently for tax purposes, often allowing for a "step-up in basis" where the inherited asset's value is adjusted to the market value on the date of the owner's death, potentially reducing capital gains taxes.

4. **Tax-Advantaged Accounts:**
In some countries, including the U.S., there are tax-advantaged accounts where you can hold crypto investments. These accounts, like Individual Retirement Accounts (IRAs), can allow for tax-free growth or tax-deferred growth, depending on the type of account. Check with a tax professional to see if crypto can be held in these

accounts in your jurisdiction.

Common Crypto Tax Mistakes to Avoid

1. **Failing to Report All Transactions:**
   Not reporting every transaction, including small trades or using crypto for purchases, can lead to tax penalties. Even seemingly insignificant transactions can have tax implications.

2. **Not Keeping Detailed Records:**
   Keeping poor records of your crypto transactions can make it difficult to accurately calculate gains and losses. It's important to track every detail for accurate tax reporting.

3. **Underestimating Taxes on Staking or Mining Rewards:**
   Failing to report income from staking, mining, or airdrops can lead to penalties. Any crypto received as rewards is taxable and must be reported.

4. **Misunderstanding "Like-Kind Exchange" Exemptions:**
   In some countries, a "like-kind exchange" might allow you to avoid capital gains taxes when swapping one type of property for another. However, as of recent years, in most jurisdictions (including the U.S.), cryptocurrencies are not considered "like-kind" property, meaning that crypto-to-crypto trades are taxable events.

Conclusion

Navigating the tax implications of crypto investments can be challenging, but understanding the basic principles of crypto taxation is essential for staying compliant and optimizing your returns. Whether it's through capital gains, staking rewards, or airdrops, tax obligations must be managed carefully. By tracking transactions, reporting income accurately, and employing tax-efficient strategies, you can minimize your liability and ensure that you remain compliant with the law. As always, consult with a tax professional to help guide you through the intricacies of crypto taxation and avoid common pitfalls.

13 The Future of Crypto and Long-Term Success

The cryptocurrency space is rapidly evolving, and the future holds both tremendous opportunities and significant challenges for investors. As we've explored throughout this book, the rules of crypto involve navigating complex technologies, markets, and regulatory environments. While the future of crypto is still unfolding, we can identify trends and principles that will guide investors toward long-term success in this dynamic space. In this final chapter, we'll reflect on the key takeaways from this book and provide insight into what the future holds for cryptocurrency.

The Increasing Role of Blockchain and Cryptocurrencies

Cryptocurrency is just one piece of the broader blockchain revolution. Blockchain technology, the underlying structure of crypto, has the potential to disrupt a wide range of industries beyond finance. Here's a look at how blockchain and crypto are poised to shape the future:

1. **Decentralization of Finance (DeFi):**
   DeFi has emerged as one of the most promising applications of blockchain technology. By removing traditional financial intermediaries such as banks, DeFi platforms offer peer-to-peer lending, borrowing, and trading, opening up financial services to millions who are unbanked or underbanked. As DeFi grows, it will likely become a significant part of the financial landscape, giving investors new opportunities for wealth generation.
2. **Integration with Traditional Finance (TradFi):**
   While DeFi is disrupting traditional finance, we are also seeing increasing integration between the two worlds. Banks, investment firms, and other financial institutions are exploring ways to incorporate blockchain into their operations, from custodial services for crypto assets to the issuance of tokenized assets. This hybrid system could lead to greater acceptance of cryptocurrencies within mainstream financial markets.

3. **Tokenization of Assets:**
   Tokenization refers to the process of converting real-world assets, such as real estate, art, and commodities, into digital tokens on a blockchain. This makes previously illiquid assets tradable on digital markets. Tokenization could revolutionize investment opportunities, making it easier for people to invest in fractional ownership of high-value assets, democratizing access to investment opportunities.
4. **NFTs and Digital Ownership:**
   Non-Fungible Tokens (NFTs) are evolving beyond digital art and collectibles. As the world embraces the concept of digital ownership, NFTs are finding use cases in industries such as real estate, gaming, and intellectual property rights. The future of NFTs is tied to the continued growth of the metaverse, where digital assets will play an integral role in virtual economies.

The Regulatory Landscape and Its Impact on Crypto

One of the most pressing issues facing the cryptocurrency market is regulation. Governments around the world are still grappling with how to regulate crypto, and these regulations will significantly shape the future of the market.

1. **Increased Government Oversight:**
   As cryptocurrencies become more mainstream, governments are under pressure to implement clearer regulations. Countries like the United States, the European Union, and China have already taken steps to regulate crypto, and more are likely to follow suit. These regulations will address issues such as tax compliance, investor protection, anti-money laundering (AML), and know-your-customer (KYC) requirements.
2. **Central Bank Digital Currencies (CBDCs):**
   In response to the rise of cryptocurrencies, many central banks are exploring the concept of Central Bank Digital Currencies (CBDCs). These government-backed digital currencies aim to provide the benefits of digital currency (speed, efficiency, transparency) while maintaining control

over monetary policy. The introduction of CBDCs could pose challenges for decentralized cryptocurrencies like Bitcoin, but it will also create new opportunities for the broader digital economy.
3. **Global Regulatory Coordination:**
   One of the main challenges in the crypto space is the lack of uniformity in regulation across countries. While some nations have embraced crypto, others have imposed restrictions or outright bans. A global regulatory framework would provide greater clarity and foster more confidence in the market. However, achieving such coordination is complex and may take years to materialize.

How Investors Can Position Themselves for Success

To thrive in the evolving world of cryptocurrency, investors need to stay informed, be adaptable, and implement sound strategies. Here are some key principles that will help you navigate the future of crypto successfully:

1. **Stay Educated and Adaptable:**
   The crypto landscape is constantly changing. New projects, innovations, and regulations emerge regularly, so it's important to stay informed. Follow credible sources, participate in communities, and continue learning to understand new trends. Adaptability is key, as what works today may not be relevant tomorrow. Successful investors will evolve alongside the market.
2. **Diversify Across Crypto and Traditional Assets:**
   While cryptocurrencies offer significant growth potential, they also come with considerable risk. A well-rounded portfolio that includes a mix of traditional assets (stocks, bonds, real estate) and crypto can help mitigate risks and provide balanced long-term growth. Diversifying within the crypto space itself, through a combination of blue-chip assets (Bitcoin, Ethereum) and emerging technologies (DeFi, NFTs), can also help smooth out volatility.
3. **Implement Sound Risk Management Practices:**
   Crypto markets are volatile, and risk management will be

crucial for long-term success. Always use tools like stop-loss orders to protect your investments from sudden market downturns, and avoid over-leveraging yourself in trades. Only invest what you can afford to lose, and be prepared for both upside and downside potential. It's also important to set realistic expectations and not chase after every hype-driven asset or short-term trend.
4. **Focus on Long-Term Vision:**
Cryptocurrencies are still in their early stages, and their long-term potential is significant. Don't get caught up in the day-to-day fluctuations of the market. Instead, focus on projects with strong fundamentals, long-term use cases, and solid development teams. Patience will be key in watching your crypto investments grow over time.
5. **Leverage Tax-Efficient Strategies:**
As we discussed in Chapter 11, understanding and planning for crypto taxes is crucial for maximizing your profits. Utilize strategies like tax-loss harvesting, holding assets long-term to take advantage of lower tax rates, and consulting with a tax professional to ensure your crypto investments are tax-efficient.

Emerging Trends to Watch in the Crypto Space

The cryptocurrency space is rapidly evolving, and new trends and technologies are constantly emerging. Here are some to keep an eye on:
1. **Interoperability:**
As the number of blockchains increases, interoperability between these networks will become more important. Projects that enable communication and seamless transactions between different blockchain platforms (like Polkadot, Cosmos, and Chainlink) will likely see significant growth.
2. **Decentralized Autonomous Organizations (DAOs):**
DAOs represent a new form of governance where decisions are made collectively by token holders rather than a central authority. As blockchain projects become more decentralized, DAOs will become increasingly important in shaping the

future of governance and financial systems.
3. **The Rise of the Metaverse:**
   The metaverse is a digital universe where users interact in virtual spaces. Cryptocurrencies and NFTs are playing a vital role in the development of the metaverse, enabling users to buy, sell, and trade virtual goods and services. As the metaverse grows, it will likely become an integral part of the global digital economy.
4. **Environmental Sustainability and Green Cryptos:**
   Environmental concerns surrounding energy consumption in cryptocurrency mining are prompting the development of more sustainable solutions. Cryptocurrencies like Ethereum, which are transitioning to energy-efficient proof-of-stake (PoS) systems, and projects focused on green energy solutions are gaining attention.

Conclusion: The Road Ahead for Crypto Investors

The future of cryptocurrency is filled with both immense opportunities and challenges. By understanding the foundational principles of crypto, staying informed about regulatory developments, and implementing sound investment strategies, you can position yourself for long-term success. The crypto landscape will continue to evolve, and the investors who thrive will be those who adapt, innovate, and remain focused on the long-term potential of this revolutionary technology.

As the world of digital assets grows, it's essential to stay proactive in learning, investing responsibly, and managing your risks. With the right mindset and strategies, the future of crypto offers a wealth of opportunities for those who are ready to navigate it.

This book has provided you with a foundation of the rules of crypto, but the journey is just beginning. Keep learning, stay curious, and continue exploring the potential of cryptocurrencies as a vehicle for wealth creation. The best is yet to come.

14 The Future of NFTs

Non-Fungible Tokens (NFTs) have been one of the most revolutionary developments in the cryptocurrency and digital asset space. Initially popularized through digital art, NFTs have since expanded into a wide variety of applications, including music, gaming, real estate, fashion, and even intellectual property. While the NFT market has witnessed extreme volatility, it is clear that the technology behind NFTs is not just a passing trend. As we look toward the future, NFTs are poised to have a transformative impact on a broad range of industries, and understanding the trends and innovations shaping the space will be critical for investors, creators, and businesses alike.

In this chapter, we will explore the future potential of NFTs, their evolving use cases, and the technological advancements that will continue to push the boundaries of what is possible. Additionally, we will discuss the challenges and opportunities that lie ahead for the NFT market and offer insights into how you can position yourself for success as this space continues to evolve.

NFTs Beyond Digital Art: A World of Possibilities

While NFTs initially gained significant attention for their use in digital art, their potential extends far beyond that. NFTs represent ownership, provenance, and scarcity in the digital world, and their applications are becoming increasingly diverse. The future of NFTs lies in their ability to bring true ownership to the digital realm, unlocking new opportunities across multiple industries. Here are some areas where NFTs are expected to have a profound impact in the future:

1. **Gaming and Virtual Worlds**

One of the most exciting and rapidly growing areas for NFTs is gaming. NFTs can revolutionize the gaming industry by enabling players to truly own their in-game assets—whether it's characters, skins, weapons, or land. These NFTs are unique, meaning that the items players acquire in a game are not just assets they can use within

that game but can also be sold, traded, or transferred to other games.
- **Play-to-Earn (P2E) Models:** The rise of play-to-earn games has demonstrated how NFTs can create new economic opportunities for gamers. By earning unique in-game assets that are tokenized as NFTs, players can monetize their gameplay in ways that were never before possible. In the future, we may see a surge in decentralized gaming ecosystems where players own a share of the game's economy, making the distinction between "work" and "play" even more blurred.
- **Interoperability Between Games:** One of the most exciting prospects is the ability to transfer NFTs between different virtual worlds and games. This could create a truly interconnected gaming ecosystem where items can be used across multiple games, enhancing the value and utility of NFTs.

2. **Real Estate and Virtual Land**

NFTs have the potential to disrupt the real estate sector by enabling the buying, selling, and transferring of virtual land. The concept of virtual land has already gained traction in platforms like Decentraland, The Sandbox, and Cryptovoxels, where users can buy and sell plots of land in virtual worlds. This virtual real estate is represented as NFTs, and its value is driven by factors like location, scarcity, and development potential.

- **Tokenization of Physical Real Estate:** Beyond the virtual realm, NFTs could also play a key role in the tokenization of physical real estate. By tokenizing real-world properties as NFTs, individuals could invest in real estate without needing to purchase an entire property. Tokenized real estate allows for fractional ownership, where multiple investors can own a share of a property, thus lowering the barrier to entry for real estate investment.

3. **Intellectual Property and Licensing**

Intellectual property (IP) has traditionally been difficult to monetize and protect, but NFTs can offer a solution by representing ownership and licensing rights. Artists, musicians, and creators can tokenize their IP, enabling them to sell, license, or even lease their digital content in a secure and verifiable way.

- **Music and Media Ownership:** In the music industry, NFTs are being used to represent ownership of music tracks, albums, and exclusive content. Artists can tokenize their music and sell it directly to fans, bypassing traditional record labels and streaming services. This direct-to-consumer model can enable creators to retain a larger share of the profits and establish closer relationships with their audience.
- **Patents and Trademarks:** NFTs could be used to represent patents, trademarks, and other intellectual property assets. By tokenizing these assets, businesses can more easily track ownership and transfer rights in a secure and transparent way. This could lead to a more efficient and streamlined process for buying and selling IP.

4. **Fashion and Digital Collectibles**

The fashion industry is increasingly embracing NFTs as a means to offer digital collectibles and virtual fashion. Virtual clothing and accessories, represented as NFTs, are already being created by high-end fashion brands like Gucci and Prada. These digital fashion items allow users to dress their avatars in virtual worlds or social media platforms like Instagram.

- **Digital Fashion and Virtual Identity:** As the metaverse continues to grow, digital fashion will play an integral role in how people express themselves online. NFTs in fashion could allow individuals to own and trade unique digital items that reflect their personal style, creating new opportunities for fashion designers, influencers, and brands.

- **Collaborations Between Fashion and Gaming:** The crossover between gaming and fashion is already happening. In the future, we could see collaborations between gaming platforms and fashion brands, creating limited-edition NFTs that are wearable both in the real world and in virtual environments. These cross-industry partnerships could open up new revenue streams for fashion brands and game developers.

5. Real-World Collectibles and Tokenized Physical Assets

While NFTs are primarily associated with digital assets, they can also be used to represent ownership of physical items. Physical assets, such as sports memorabilia, luxury goods, and even rare physical collectibles, can be tokenized as NFTs, enabling easier tracking of authenticity and ownership.

- **Tokenization of High-Value Assets:** NFTs could be used to prove the authenticity and ownership of luxury items such as watches, fine art, and rare collectibles. By attaching an NFT to a physical asset, the buyer receives a verifiable, immutable proof of ownership, ensuring the item is genuine and helping to prevent counterfeiting.

The Role of Smart Contracts and Decentralized Autonomous Organizations (DAOs)

The future of NFTs will be heavily intertwined with the development of smart contracts and decentralized governance through DAOs. Smart contracts are self-executing contracts with the terms of the agreement directly written into code. These contracts are automated and immutable, meaning they can execute transactions without intermediaries.

- **Automated Royalties and Secondary Sales:** One of the most powerful aspects of NFTs is the ability to set up automated royalty payments. Creators can program NFTs

with a smart contract that ensures they receive a percentage of sales every time the NFT is resold on secondary markets. This provides a continuous revenue stream for creators and ensures they are fairly compensated for their work.
- **DAOs for NFT Projects:** DAOs are decentralized organizations governed by token holders rather than a central authority. In the future, NFT projects could be governed by DAOs, where community members have a say in the development, distribution, and management of NFTs. This decentralized governance model ensures that decisions are made collectively, promoting transparency and fairness in the NFT ecosystem.

The Challenges Facing NFTs and the Road Ahead

While NFTs have tremendous potential, they also face several challenges that need to be addressed as the space matures:

1. **Environmental Concerns:**
   NFTs and blockchain technology often rely on energy-intensive consensus mechanisms like Proof of Work (PoW). This has led to concerns about the environmental impact of NFT minting and transactions. However, efforts are underway to transition to more sustainable systems, such as Proof of Stake (PoS), which are expected to reduce the energy consumption associated with NFTs.
2. **Regulation and Legal Framework:**
   As the NFT market grows, regulatory clarity will be essential to protect investors and creators. Governments will likely introduce regulations to address issues such as copyright, intellectual property rights, taxation, and anti-money laundering. Clear regulations will help establish trust and ensure the long-term viability of the NFT market.
3. **Scalability and Network Congestion:**
   The current infrastructure of blockchain networks, such as Ethereum, can struggle with scalability, particularly during periods of high demand. High transaction fees and network congestion can make it difficult to mint, buy, or sell NFTs efficiently. However, advancements in Layer 2 solutions, sidechains, and alternative blockchain networks are

addressing these scalability issues.

Conclusion: A Bright Future for NFTs

The future of NFTs is incredibly bright, with the technology poised to disrupt industries ranging from art and entertainment to real estate and finance. NFTs are enabling a new era of digital ownership, where creators and consumers alike can engage with assets in ways that were never before possible. As the technology matures, we can expect NFTs to evolve into more sophisticated and integrated tools that provide utility and value across diverse sectors.

For investors, creators, and businesses, now is the time to explore the potential of NFTs. The opportunities in the NFT space are vast, and by staying informed and adapting to the changing landscape, you can position yourself at the forefront of this digital revolution.

Conclusion: Embracing the Future of Crypto

Cryptocurrency has moved from a niche technological experiment to a global financial force that is shaping the future of money, investment, and decentralization. In this book, we have covered the essential rules, strategies, and concepts that will help you navigate the crypto space successfully. From understanding blockchain fundamentals to managing tax obligations and positioning yourself for long-term growth, these insights are designed to equip you with the knowledge to thrive in this rapidly evolving ecosystem.

As we look to the future, the opportunities in cryptocurrency are vast. The rise of decentralized finance (DeFi), blockchain innovations, NFTs, and the potential integration of digital currencies into mainstream financial systems present tremendous potential for wealth creation and growth. However, navigating this space requires a combination of knowledge, discipline, and adaptability. By staying informed, understanding the risks, and employing sound strategies, you can maximize the potential of your crypto investments while minimizing the associated risks.

The cryptocurrency market is inherently volatile, but it is also filled with long-term opportunities for those who take a thoughtful, calculated approach. Remember that success in crypto doesn't come from chasing short-term gains or following the crowd—it comes from a clear understanding of the fundamentals, ongoing learning, and strategic decision-making.

As you move forward, keep in mind the principles we've covered:

- The importance of understanding blockchain technology and the assets you invest in.

- The need to have a well-diversified portfolio, balancing risk and reward.

- The significance of securing your assets and staying compliant with regulatory guidelines.

- The necessity of managing your taxes efficiently and seeking professional advice when needed.

The road to success in the crypto world is not without its challenges, but with patience, perseverance, and the right knowledge, it can be incredibly rewarding. Cryptocurrency is more than just a trend—it is the future of finance, offering new ways to transact, invest, and create value in the world.

This book has equipped you with the tools you need to succeed in the crypto space, but it is just the beginning of your journey. The world of cryptocurrency will continue to evolve, and as an investor, it's crucial that you evolve with it. Stay curious, stay informed, and, most importantly, stay engaged. The future of crypto is exciting, and it's a future that you can be a part of—creating wealth, driving innovation, and contributing to the financial systems of tomorrow.

Your journey in crypto starts now. Embrace the opportunity, stay focused, and prepare to be part of one of the most transformative revolutions in the financial world.

Thank you for reading, and best of luck on your crypto journey!